GW01117714

IN TOUCH WITH MY ROOTS
A CREATIVE JOURNEY THROUGH KERALA

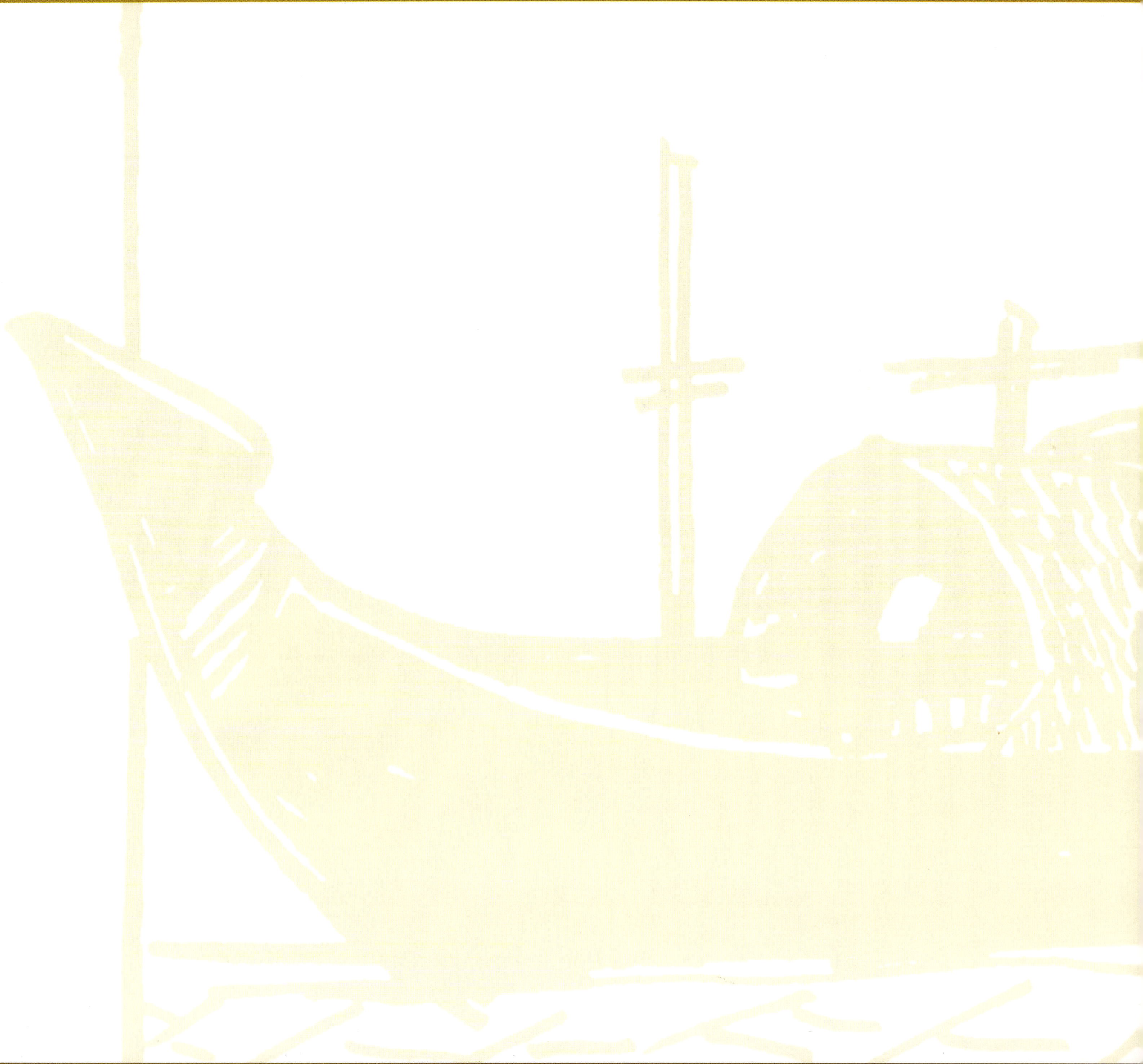

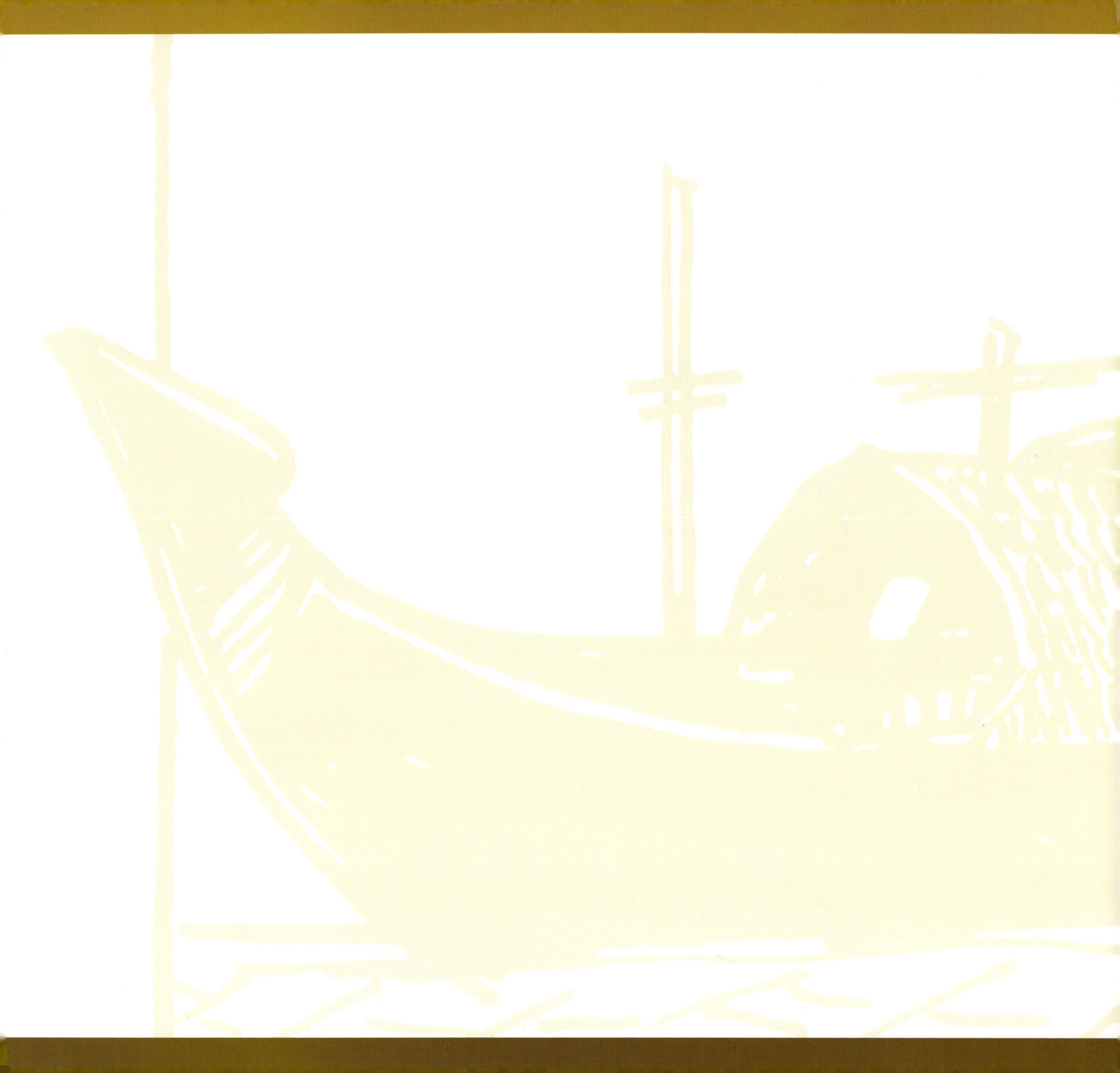

IN TOUCH WITH MY ROOTS
A CREATIVE JOURNEY THROUGH KERALA

Yusuf Arakkal

PENGUIN ENTERPRISE
Published by the Penguin Group
Penguin Books India Pvt. Ltd, 11 Community Centre, Panchsheel Park, New Delhi 110 017, India
Penguin Group (USA) Inc., 375 Hudson Street, New York, New York 10014, USA
Penguin Group (Canada), 90 Eglinton Avenue East, Suite 700, Toronto, Ontario, M4P 2Y3, Canada (a division of Pearson Penguin Canada Inc.)
Penguin Books Ltd, 80 Strand, London WC2R 0RL, England
Penguin Ireland, 25 St Stephen's Green, Dublin 2, Ireland (a division of Penguin Books Ltd)
Penguin Group (Australia), 250 Camberwell Road, Camberwell, Victoria 3124, Australia (a division of Pearson Australia Group Pty Ltd)
Penguin Group (NZ), cnr Airborne and Rosedale Roads, Albany, Auckland 1310, New Zealand (a division of Pearson New Zealand Ltd)
Penguin Group (South Africa) (Pty) Ltd, 24 Sturdee Avenue, Rosebank, Johannesburg 2196, South Africa
Penguin Books Ltd, Registered Offices: 80 Strand, London WC2R 0RL, England

First published in Penguin Enterprise by Penguin Books India 2006

Copyright © Yusuf Arakkal 2006

All rights reserved

10 9 8 7 6 5 4 3 2 1

ISBN 13: 978-0-14306-225-7 ISBN 10: 0-14306-225-5

Book Design by Prints of Desire
Typeset by Prints of Desire
Printed at Ajanta Offset & Packaging Ltd., New Delhi

This book is sold subject to the condition that it shall not, by way of trade or otherwise, be lent, resold, hired out, or otherwise circulated without the publisher's prior written consent in any form of binding or cover other than that in which it is published and without a similar condition including this condition being imposed on the subsequent purchaser and without limiting the rights under copyright reserved above, no part of this publication may be reproduced, stored in or introduced into a retrieval system, or transmitted in any form or by any means (electronic, mechanical, photocopying, recording or otherwise), without the prior written permission of both the copyright owner and the above-mentioned publisher of this book.

Foreword

Since time immemorial, Kerala, land extraordinaire, has been enchanting the world with her singular beauty and charm. The lush landscapes, the enchanting monsoons, the clean, scented air . . . all inspiring many a heart to look at life in a new light. There's something about the land that stirs up a sense of belonging. And those who are touched by Kerala's beauty and vivacity surrender their hearts to her forever, eventually building a deep bond with the land that lasts a lifetime.

This exceptional splendour is perhaps what helped Kerala nurture many illustrious poets and painters, writers and film makers. And this is perhaps what made Yusuf Arakkal what he is today. Like every Keralite, Yusuf carries with him a bit of the land wherever he goes - the spice-scent of the hills, the invigorating smell of damp earth, the quiet charm of the villages, the comforting greenery . . . constantly seeking the serenity of the landscape to enrich his mindscape.

Nobody could have painted a better picture of Kerala than Yusuf Arakkal. For he gives you not just an insider's view of the land, but also an objective view of an 'outsider' - having left home as a teenager looking for creative freedom and individual identity. In earthy reds, ochres and blacks, Yusuf brilliantly captures the myriad moods and images of this emerald State. His is an eye that looks beyond the obvious and each stroke of his brush mirrors the rare bonding he has with the land, thus sketching a portrait of God's Own Country like never before. Which also explains why Kerala Tourism decided to associate itself with this prolific painter in this remarkable endeavour.

We hope this intimate homeward journey will inspire readers to set out on a new journey to God's Own Country. Bon voyage.

kerala
God's Own Country

'Kerala is colours – magnificient colours,' George Devlin, my Scottish artist-friend, once said. He was referring to the myriad hues that fuse with the natural green of nature, bestowing upon it the well-deserved epithet of God's Own Country. And all around hundreds of flags in varied hues – identities of the ever-sprouting political parties – that also seem to merge in synchronicity whenever Kerala is in crisis.

Kerala – a land so full of contradictions, yet, paradoxically a confluence of racial, ethnic and religious strains. Matthai and Mammuty celebrate the Onam festival with the same fervour as Raman Nair or Appukuttan. They wear the same *mundus* and put on their *thundus* on their head to protect themselves from the rain or the sun and amazingly speak the same language – Malayalam.

Speaking of Malayalam, it is a language with a great literary tradition and a highly developed modern literature. Thunjath Ezhuthachan, Poonthanam, Vallathol, G. Sankarakurup, Balamaniyamma, Kumaran Asan, Changampuzha are all household names. Bhasheer, Thakazhi, Kesvadev, Ponkunnam Varky, Uroob, O.V. Vijayan belong to a great modern literary tradition that is now carried forward by names like M.T. Vasudevan Nair, VKN, Punathil Kunhabdulla, ONV

Kurup, Anand, M.N. Vijayan, Sukumar Azheekode, Mukundan, Kamala Das, Sukatha Kumari – just to mention a few literary geniuses of Kerala. C.V. Balakrishnan, P. Surendran, Prabhakaran, Balachandran Chullikad are some of the prominent writers among the young generation.

Kerala is a land where creative people are highly respected and even worshipped. It has gifted many artists to the Indian art world. Raja Ravi Varma who pioneered the oil painting tradition in India and popularized mythological themes, became a household name throughout the country. Among modern artists the late K.C.S. Pannikar is a highly respected name. K.G. Subramaniyan, A. Ramachandran, Viswanathan, Akkithan, Achuthan Kudallur, Nandagopal, Balan Nambiar, Kanayi, Namboodri, Devan, Babu Xavier, Haridasan, Douglas, Radhakrishnan, P. Gopinath, Azis T.M., John C.F., Anuradha Nalappat, Krishnamachari Bose, Riaz Komu, Jitish Kallat and numerous others are Kerala's contribution to Indian contemporary art.

I must have been hardly ten years old when – the old man sitting next to me on the wayside teashop bench began his story . . .

'Rapayyi Mappila sold coconut oil at our local weekend market. He must have been in his late sixties at that time. But very sturdy. I was buying fish next door when I heard the commotion at Rappayi Mappila's store. I saw four mean and very menacing-looking men shouting abuses at him.

He merely smiled and asked them to leave. But suddenly one of them pounced on him. Rappayi Mappila stood there like a rock and just pointed his index finger at them, as if shooting a pistol. You know what happened next?. . .' the old man continued, with a bewildered expression on his face, 'they all fell down one by one like trees chopped down!'
'That is *choondani murmam*,' interrupted the teashop owner, pointing a finger at me.

Choondani murmam was a martial art trick that hardly anyone knew of anymore. It is said that one could bring an adversary down at twenty feet away by just pointing a finger at him. Such feats of martial art may be related as stories now but they all had a factual basis. Many great martial art exponents are history now but their memories are kept alive through stories.

Mystery and mythology are indeed the essence of the birth of Kerala. It is believed that, with the intention of gifting a large stretch of land to the Brahmins, the great sage Parashuram threw his weapon – an axe – into the Arabian Sea. Land sprang up along the entire distance the axe travelled. And so was born Kerala!

The splendour of nature and its vagaries continue to astound visitors to the state. Starting from the dark green grass – so dark that you feel the colour will come out on your fingers if you so much as touch it – to the leaves in all shades of green despite the gruelling heat and humidity, the monsoons bring a startling change of striking emerald, viridian and sap green to the landscape. And against this overpowering beauty of nature, zipping past on the roads can be seen chauffer-driven Mercedes-Benz cars with men in their Hawaii chappals (seemingly the favoured footwear)!

My on and off romance with Kerala has been a continuous exercise since the age of fifteen, when I first left for greener (!) pastures. But I never really left my native land in spirit, just as I do not think any Malayali can ever. In my case I went out searching for creative freedom which I found lacking within the traditional confines of my family. Whether I was correct in thinking so is only something I can reflect on in hindsight, but at that time, it seemed to be the 'ideal solution' to a rebellious fifteen-year-old looking for his own identity. However, romancing the land of my birth was far from over: my family, my relatives and most of all – my roots being deeply ingrained in Kerala's soil. The dark grass may have grown over but it remained there all right.

Rediscovery

My return to Kerala was not a journey backwards to rediscover my native place as a resident, but to feel and understand the changes and evolution that had taken place – the visible and the not so apparent. As part of a creative journey. I did not intend to rediscover what I had never lost. A new sense of comprehension was more like it. Here was I – a non-resident Keralite who loved his home town but found it difficult to comprehend the psyche of the locals and his land.

There is a strong sense of belonging as I drive down the winding, narrow roads. Kerala is the only place in the entire world that boasts a hundred per cent literacy. It is justifiably proud of its almost garbage-free zone and a prosperous race that seeks out opportunities and is ever ready to take on new challenges. The Malayali will travel to far-off lands, to deserts and the arctic regions to seek his fortune. There is hardly any place in the world where you do not encounter a Malyali. There is an often-told joke of how, when Neil Armstrong landed on the moon, a Malayali approached him selling tea!

The narrow roads are an experience in themselves – a driver's paradise and a pedestrian's nightmare. My driver Faizal was earlier used to driving the Chief Minister's car, with its blaring siren, rotating red light and his foot pressed on the accelerator. I too have a car with a red light on top, courtesy the Tourism Department – a Contessa – and he thinks that he is still driving the Chief Minister! Kerala can train many a Schumacher on its smooth (hic) curving roads! But the Formula 1 race is the last thing on my mind as I hold on for dear life while the driver navigates the hair-bend turns and we miss lorries and buses by micro inches. My thoughts move from the inane to the metaphysical as we inch closer towards Wynad and Vythri. The fragrance from the coffee plantations accompanies us as we move. Cinnamon, pepper and other spices fill the air with their aroma. The air is cooler, probably the coolest in an otherwise humid Kerala.

'We are now cooler than Ooty and Kodaikanal,' one of the men on the coffee plantations informs me proudly. Seeing that I look skeptical, he swears that it has even been mentioned in the newspaper. 'And, of course, we are zero pollution,' he grins smugly. I can't help agreeing as we move down the untarred road that leads to the resort at Vythri. The folk here seem to have taken their love for nature a little too far by not tarring the roads. Adventure is all very well, but a little comfort never hurt any, and with my driver never slowing down, the loose stones literally fly in all directions. Deer, bison and wild birds roam the roads fearlessly; I guess they are used to the passing vehicles by now. A lone elephant can be seen in the thicket. This area is home to probably the largest elephant population in south India. The adjoining forests of Bandipur and MM hills serve as migratory homes, I am told.

We have started out from Bangalore early in the morning. At Mysore, my friend Joseph who is accompanying me as far as Calicut, and I have breakfast at another friend, Chandasakar's residence. Chandasakar is the Commissioner of Police, Mysore.

Putting a brush or pencil to canvas is something I've been itching to do from the moment we started out. This is the place that was teeming with tribals during pre-independence days. They led their own little revolts against the British, and some were even successful. One tribal, a great martyr now, even has a tree dedicated to him. Folklore has it that he was hanged from that very tree by the British. Iron chains hang over the branches till today. Probably symbolic of bondage. A permanent reminder. Another famous icon in these parts is Pazhassi Raja, also a rebel, known as the Lion of Kerala. The cave that he used as a hideout till he was discovered by the British is today an important monument. What strikes me as I hear such tales of heroism is that even though the British managed to get them all, the rebellions continued. That same rebellious spirit still manifests in small gatherings of men and women shouting slogans on the road. Keralites just don't take anything lying down. They are always protesting about one thing or other. While the awareness level is all very well, it makes life on an everyday basis a little difficult to get used to, especially if you are visiting the state.

The political awareness in the state is awesome. I am yet to see any other place in the world where the awareness level is this high. Children barely out of their cradles have strong political affiliations and are members of some Bala Sangham or other. I am still to decide whether this is a good thing or not. My guide, Mr Krshna Varrier, assures me that it helps people to be aware of politics when they are young! I am not very sure of that. Why then the interest in politics? Precisely for the same reason, he explains. Not all politics are bad, my young photographer Mohan intervenes. Well, I am not very sure about that too. 'How far is the resort?' I change the subject, fearing a political discussion in the car.

The common folk in Kerala might not lead a grand life; however they are happy with their *choru* and *meen* curry – rice and fish and *pappadams*. Sending their children to school is their first priority. The early mornings are a delight. Hundreds and hundreds of children marching on the sidewalks – uniforms, coloured clothes, shoes, chappals, *mundus* and shirts – anything goes. No uniformity here except that they all carry books and bags. In places like Kannur, Wynad and Calicut where Muslims are present in large numbers, the little girls with *hijabs*, traditional scarves worn on the head, remind me of the little penguins in Antarctica, as shown on the National Geographic TV channel. Trotting down the road, giggling and whispering, their naivete brings to the fore the age of innocence, reminiscent of the Garden of Eden, before the entry of Adam and Eve!

The resort at Vythri can be likened to a modern Garden of Eden. Beautiful rope bridges that lurch and sway as you walk over them . . . a copse of bamboo trees through which you have to manoeuvre your way carefully . . . a gigantic bird from the bush which suddenly gives you company on your balcony . . . the sound of the gushing stream beside the window as I sit down to do a watercolour of a tree, a branch of which overhangs my cottage . . . the bird continues to hum at the window till I fall asleep. This is surely the stuff that fairy tales are made of. And it is all here! In the morning, the beauty of the surroundings presents a new splendour. I finish several sketches before leaving – with every intention of returning here.

In spite of modernization, the lifestyle of the people does not really seem to have changed. They continue to live in tiled-roof houses, barring a few concrete horrors, and go about their work with enviable calm. The Taj group of hotels might have put up six spectacular hotels in the state to cope with the sudden deluge of tourists. But the *chaya kada*, the local tea stall, still continues to be the hub where world politics are discussed, the performances of leaders are scrutinized and opinions are aired vociferously. The man who pours your tea could be Bapputy or Baskaran or Thomachan – I come across all three – rather like a movie on national integration! Tourists may have replaced a Hawaii with Kerala in their mind's eye, but for the resident Keralite, life goes on mindless of the intrusion of black suits and bikinis. There may be the odd chance of a local accosting you about your age, your place of birth, your income, your native land – in short, just about everything. And if you ask why he needs all this information, he will probably merely shrug his Malayali shoulder and walk on!

Vythri has a calming effect that most places can only aspire for. It is probably the air or the height that does it. I can visualize congregations of artists, poets and writers producing superb works amidst such environs. I know I can paint here endlessly without a care in the world. Joseph and I go boating in a native *thoni* in the serene Pookode Lake, and I do a couple of sketches, mainly of boatmen. However, like all good things come to an end, we must leave behind the picturesque cottages, tribal huts and swaying bridges and move on.

From Vythri, we head towards Kannur – believed to be the land of my ancestors even though I was born in Chowghat. The Arakkals were very well known and powerful in this area at one time. They still are, though they are not involved in politics anymore. The Arakkal Ali Rajas were the only Muslim royal family of Kerala, though they descended from a Hindu ruling family. The last of the royals – the Bibi of the family – lives in an ordinary home with her brother, the son of the last Sultan. The palace called the Arakkal Kettu, now restored with assistance from the State, is walking distance from her house. To think that I am a descendent invokes a sense of pride in me, even though it is a trifle misplaced. Meeting the Bibi is a nostalgic experience and we converse endlessly. Her nieces and nephews live within a common compound close by. There is absolutely no trace of royalty here. Most of the younger generation has entered different walks of life, with many going to the Middle East, where all ambitious Keralites go in search of a prosperous future. Some have become IT professionals. Their mothers stay back, guarding their properties, waiting for sons and families that will never return, having got used to the fast cars and opulence of richer nations.

The Muthappan Temple at Parassinakadavu is another marvel rediscovered. Here the Theyyam – a traditional folk dance (probably one of the oldest ritual dance forms in the world – a fusion of art, music and theatre) is performed everyday, at dawn and at dusk. Hundreds of devotees and tourists gather to witness this grand spectacle. The red masked dancers with thee *pandhams*, fire sticks, look ferocious and majestic. Along with them numerous street dogs can be seen around the temple compounds. The locals relate a story connecting the dogs to the temple, a story that I'm sure I've heard in my childhood but can't recollect. I don't however stay for a second narration. I am tempted to do a watercolour but decide against it – there is no point in copying a piece of great art in itself. It's time to move and I'm on my way.

I can't help wondering as we move on how things might have been different if I had just stayed on instead of giving in to the lure of moving to Bangalore. I would perhaps have become a football player – another great passion of Malayalis – I was a good football player in my high school days and even captained the junior team. In fact I was so good that I was nicknamed Thangaraj – after the great Olympian goalkeeper. However, moving to Bangalore is a decision I have never had reason to regret. Bangalore has been a wonderful home to me – a loving foster mother – and everything I am worth today – I owe to Bangalore. When I think of a native land, I think of two places and not one.

The ever-winding roads present no problem to my driver Faizal, who hardly relaxes on the accelerator. One after another, the terracotta red of tiled roofs streaks past the greens: all the houses are the same, the only variance being in the size of their compounds. The traffic begins to thicken and more hoardings and more stores begin to appear. The ever-present human population on the roads becomes denser. We are approaching the historical citadel that has witnessed the coming and going of numerous races – Arabs, Europeans, Africans, Mongols, Chinese and others.

Calicut, as it was called by the British, is now Kozhikode, its original name. They say that King Solomon's subjects travelled all the way here to trade in spices. But what makes Kozhikode important for us is that Vasco da Gama landed there in 1498 at Kappad Beach. Incidentally, *kappadu* in neighbouring Karnataka means help, which must have been exactly what Vasco's three vessels would have wanted after a long search for land. The unique formation of rocks that juts out into the sea is a geographical marvel. At dawn, the sea is calm and the early morning rays of the sun highlight the rock formation. I sketch the various shapes jutting out into the Arabian Sea.

I behold another marvellous sight: When the fishermen return from the sea, little shrimps cling to their nets – hundreds and hundreds of them, representing a union of sea victims. I wonder – are they too politically aware creatures? My thoughts wander while sketching a boat lying on its side in the sand, waiting for the fishermen to move it to the sea for its daily chore.

My thoughts are disrupted by someone tugging at my tee shirt. It is a young child with distinct Arab features. 'You only draw boats?' the innocent voice is almost drowned in the roar of the sea as it awakens.
'Well, I do sketch other things too.' I show him my sketch pad. A few more children gather around me.
'Then draw me please,' he says in an unsure voice. His innocent eyes however demand I sketch him. Which is what I do.
'It is just like him,' is the general consensus.
'But his eyes are not that slanted.' A dissident voice – typical of a Malyali.

North Malabar, stretching from Kannur to Wynad and Kozhikode, is an area of Muslim majority unlike the rest of Kerala. The girls in their *hijabs*, curious, yet shy. The man on the street is equally curious but there is nothing shy in his demeanour. He wants to know everything, including your date of birth. A resident Keralite can sniff out an outsider immediately even if the latter can speak the language fluently. Foreigners are ignored as if the locals know better than to drill those who are merely tourists.

I am supposed to go to Tasara, a weaving centre on the outskirts of Kozhikode. Tasara has been an artists' camp, where the latter have created works of art later woven into priceless threads. Unfortunately certain scheduling problems result in my visit being cancelled.

The road from Kozhikode to Cochin is a long and humid one. The paddy fields exist in harmony with STD booths and Internet parlours, the five-star hotels with the fishermen's huts. Kerala is for everyone. En route is Thrissur where the majestic Pooram Festival takes place. Since I am visiting at the wrong time of the year, I will miss out on the *panchavadyam*, the caparisoned elephants, and, of course, the famous fireworks I so enjoyed as a boy.

From Thrissur we head towards the seaside for Guruvayoor, one of the most famous temples in India. When we reach the west gate of the temple town, my thoughts go back to the countless days I spent here as a boy – my high school was just a kilometre away. Many of my childhood friends – the Nairs and Namboodiris – have told me about the paintings inside the temple. But I cannot enter as it is taboo for a non-Hindu. My guide Varrier goes in to pray and brings *prasadam* for all of us. I have a special affiliation with this temple. My grandmother who was a staunch Muslim, told me that I was born on the same day and time as Lord Krishna, who is known here as Guruvayoorappan, and is the presiding deity of the temple. This temple follows every rule in the book seriously and is perhaps the most revered temple in the south, after Tirupati and Sabarimala.

As we move towards Cochin and Ernakulam (twin cities) – a man-made island, a thriving harbour and a shipyard that builds modern sea-going vessels – the paddy fields and coconut palms begin to diminish. Smart stores, shopping complexes, wider roads with dividers and a more Westernized population begin to emerge. Girls in jeans and boys in shorts – Cochin is cosmopolitan. But it is old-world too, with its Jew Town, the Cathedral, the Dutch Palace and the Chinese fishing nets.

It is believed that the Chinese fishing nets were brought to India during the rule of Kublai Khan. A Chinese net looks like it will disintegrate any minute and yet, it works and how. Loads of struggling fish are pulled into the nets with every pull. The beach is a tourist's delight. 'Catch Fish – Eat Fish' proclaims a board. This doesn't imply that you go and catch the fish; it gives you the option of selecting the fish you want and getting it cooked, in Kerala style, if you like. The Arabian Sea is in its full splendour at Cochin – a beautiful shade of luminescent orange and blue at twilight. The sea has seen them come and go – the prince and the pauper, the poet, the politician and the painter. I grew up on the sands of the shore of the Arabian Sea – sculpted the sand, drew countless pictures of the fishing boats and occasional dhows that came from Arabia, watched the sea gulls fly towards the horizon in the evening sun that slowly melted gold into the emerald water.

The synagogue almost takes your breath away. Old and frail, it stands like a fading flag still heralding a bygone era of opulence. The small crowded road that leads to the synagogue in Jew Town is dotted with old Jewish houses, and numerous shops selling artifacts and antiques. Sadly only five or six Jewish families are still around. The remaining Jews have relocated to America or Israel. The old lady who sells beautifully embroidered tablecloths is one of the few original Jews left, though you would find it difficult to believe since she speaks English, Malayalam and Hebrew with equal fluency. In fact, her English is now accented with Malayalam. The floor of the synagogue is fitted with blue and white Chinese tiles. At first glance they look the same, but take a closer look – no two tiles are alike. There are at least 1,000 tiles here. The pulpit is fitted with brass, and the chandeliers lend it a grand air. A religion that gave birth to two others is celebrated here by a handful of followers, who still observe Sabbath on Saturdays when the synagogue is closed. Mohan goes around to find the best view for photographs. I sit almost in the middle of the road to get a clear view for my watercolour. A small crowd gathers around me, a few directing the traffic so as not to break my concentration. I complete the watercolour in about half an hour and an ad hoc committee promptly puts it out on display on the sidewalk for passers-by to admire. In Kerala, there is a committee for everything! I am not used to signing many autographs, but that day I have to. To be an artist in Kerala is something really big!

For me the synagogue is a spiritual relic with a spirit that refuses to die and continues to live on. The Dutch palace is a beautiful structure adorned with mural paintings and stories from the Puranas. Bolghatty Island and Wellingdon Island, with their old palaces, picturesque gardens and ancient scriptures are also a draw for tourists, who are overawed by their sheer beauty. The man on the street takes it all for granted since it is in his backstreet, so to speak. I first visited the Mattancheri palace with M.F. Husain when I was an art student.

After the pulsating rhythm of Cochin, Alapuzha is like a soothing balm. Its quiet pace seems to regularize the smooth flow of the backwaters again. Alapuzha is often called the Venice of the East. A natural flow of the tributaries into the river, lakes and sea have created endless kilometres of backwaters in this area. The serenity is at times disturbed by the whirring sound of a motorboat. The houseboats do brisk business, with all the tourists flocking for a backwater cruise which may be for a day or more. The houseboat moving unhurriedly through the water passes women washing clothes, children bathing, ducks gliding by and farmers baling hay in their backyards. At times, the children wave out, but more often than not, they ignore this steady stream of traffic in the backwaters.

Once a thriving port and trade centre, the long peer, now almost defunct, juts out into the sea in a dilapidated condition. We walk cautiously on the rotting timber. I have to sit practically at the end to get a clear view of the old warehouses that I sketch; a couple of tourists slouching against the faded walls of a warehouse bespeak its lost glory.

You can stop for a drink of coconut water. Most houseboats are equipped with their own cooks and kitchens. Lying down and gazing at the stars in the clear sky, as the waves sing you a lullaby to the rocking rhythm of the boat, and the smell of toddy wafts through your nostrils, is the closest you can come to heaven on earth.

Alapuzha has no claim to fame other than it was an erstwhile prosperous harbour town. Its palaces, temples, church, and even the beautiful beaches fade in comparison to the bounty that nature has bestowed the place with. I cannot help but notice the enormous showrooms selling umbrellas – they are akin to huge shopping malls, with their glass doors, window displays et al. The wrath of the South West monsoon is something that the rest of the country can only wonder at. During the endless days of torrential downpours, the umbrella stores make a killing.

Closer to Alapuzha is the Marari Beach Resort – an agreeable mix of modern amenities and ethnic traditions apparent in the architecture and the sprawling coconut grove. I walk down to the beach at the rise of the first rays of the sun. The fishermen of Mararikulam village are at the beach preparing to leave for the day's fishing expedition. I approach one of them named Philip and request him to pose for me. He agrees readily and actually calls the others to watch me sketching him. Everybody scrutinizes the final outcome and Philip asks me to sketch his friend George too and give him the drawing. He tells me that he too is an artist – 'but I can only draw boats'.

Back to the road – this time we head towards Thiruvananthapuram and straight to the tourists' paradise – Kovalam. Ayurvedic massages, white sandy beaches, aqua blue seas – it's time for the magic word – relaxation. On the way, however, there is a brief stopover at the Krishnapuram palace at Kayamkulam. The beautiful mural paintings here have withstood the test of time. Gajendra Moksham is the theme of the mural which is done in the Kerala traditional style and is reminiscent of its splendid counterparts at the famous Mattancheri Palace at Cochin. It depicts the story of King Indradumnan who was a great devotee of Lord Krishna. Cursed by the sage Agasthya, he was turned into an elephant and forced to live in the forest waiting for moksha and consequent transformation to his old self. While there, he went to drink water in a lotus pond. Huhu, a *gandharva*, who had been cursed to become a crocodile, lived in that pond. The crocodile caught hold of the elephant's leg and would not let it go. The elephant prayed to Lord Krishna who appeared in the form of Maha Vishnu and transformed both Indraduman and Huhu back to their original selves.

The pictorial spacing and narration is masterly and the sombre colours are a feast for the eyes. The mural does, however, need some urgent restoration work, priceless as it is. The adjoining museum houses paintings, statues and other works of that period. The museum keeper points to a rather grim statue of Kali, the angry avatar of the Mother Goddess, and says: 'She is Bhadrakali – and you see many ladies who look very similar to this when they get angry or can't get their way.' The open hair, the bloodshot eyes and the terror that Kali strikes are indeed petrifying! The traditional *nallukattu* structure, comprising an open courtyard and four surrounding verandahs opening into it, is made of rich old wood, and has been well preserved. 'We even have old Buddha statues, just like the ones that were destroyed in Afghanistan,' the keeper states proudly.

After that stopover, we make our way to Thiruvananthapuram (called Trivandrum by the British), the hub of politics. Steeped in history, the erstwhile and the current rulers belong to Thiruvananthapuram. Though the pulse rate of the city is not as fast as that of Cochin, it bespeaks power. As we pass the city and move on to Kovalam, anything more idyllic than this is difficult to imagine. The bluest of skies, the coolest of breezes – tourists sunbathe from dawn to dusk. At first glance, Kovalam reminds you of Goa, but only just. It has a definite character of its own. Backpackers to chartered-flight tourists – Kovalam has them all. Many come in search of nirvana; others for the Ayurvedic treatments that have hit the world in recent times. The sea, the breeze and the sand are the only constants and their beauty never diminishes. Every time you look at the landscape, you are spellbound at the marvels of nature and humbled at the insignificance of man in the larger scheme of things.

The fishermen here still use the catamaran – an amazing contraption of a boat created by just two wooden logs tied together with ropes. The name must be derived from the Malayalam words *kettiya maram* – simply wood tied together. It is difficult to believe that fishermen venture into a turbulent sea in this! Mohan begins taking pictures of the woman selling tender coconuts, while I sketch the catamaran. Meanwhile, the woman questions the purpose of taking her pictures and maintains that she must get her share of money. She certainly is on the right track!

The Shree Chitra Gallery at Trivandrum is a must-see – it houses some masterpieces of the Roerichs – both father and son, and brilliant works of Raja Ravi Varma. I feel humbled to look at my work or myself in the presence of such illustrious art.

The Padmanabhapuram Palace is another piece of history that takes your mind back in time to appreciate that while the rest of the country was embroiled in warfare, the royal family here was promoting and patronizing the finest artists in the state. Even today, I know several youngsters of the Varma clan who continue with their artistic pursuits, having accepted the merger of the princely kingdoms with the state, gracefully.

After my cup overflows with culture, Kovalam with its three crescent-shaped beaches, is to me like a sanctuary. Tomorrow is another day. Work, stress, problems of the real world – everything awaits me on my return. But for now it's the sanctuary that matters. I can revel in the waves, the breeze, the sun – in a country blessed by the gods themselves.

▶ Chinese fishing net, Kochi
10" x 14", watercolour, 2001

▲ Fishermen in their boat, Kappad
10" x 14", pen and ink drawing, 2001

Chinese Fishing Net, Kochi

◀ Vythiri Resort
   10" x 14", pen and ink drawing, 2001

▶ A farmer, Wynad
   10" x 14", watercolour, 2001

FARMER VUNAD. 15·1·2001

Pushcart Puller
Trichur.

▼ Varghese Mappila, Thrissur
10" x 14", pen and ink drawing, 2001

◀ Push cart puller, Thrissur
10" x 14", watercolour, 2001

Arakkal kettu
Cannur · 13-1-2001

◀ Part of the Arakkal Palace
   10" x 14", pen and ink drawing, 2001

▶ The synagogue, Kochi
   10" x 14", watercolour, 2001

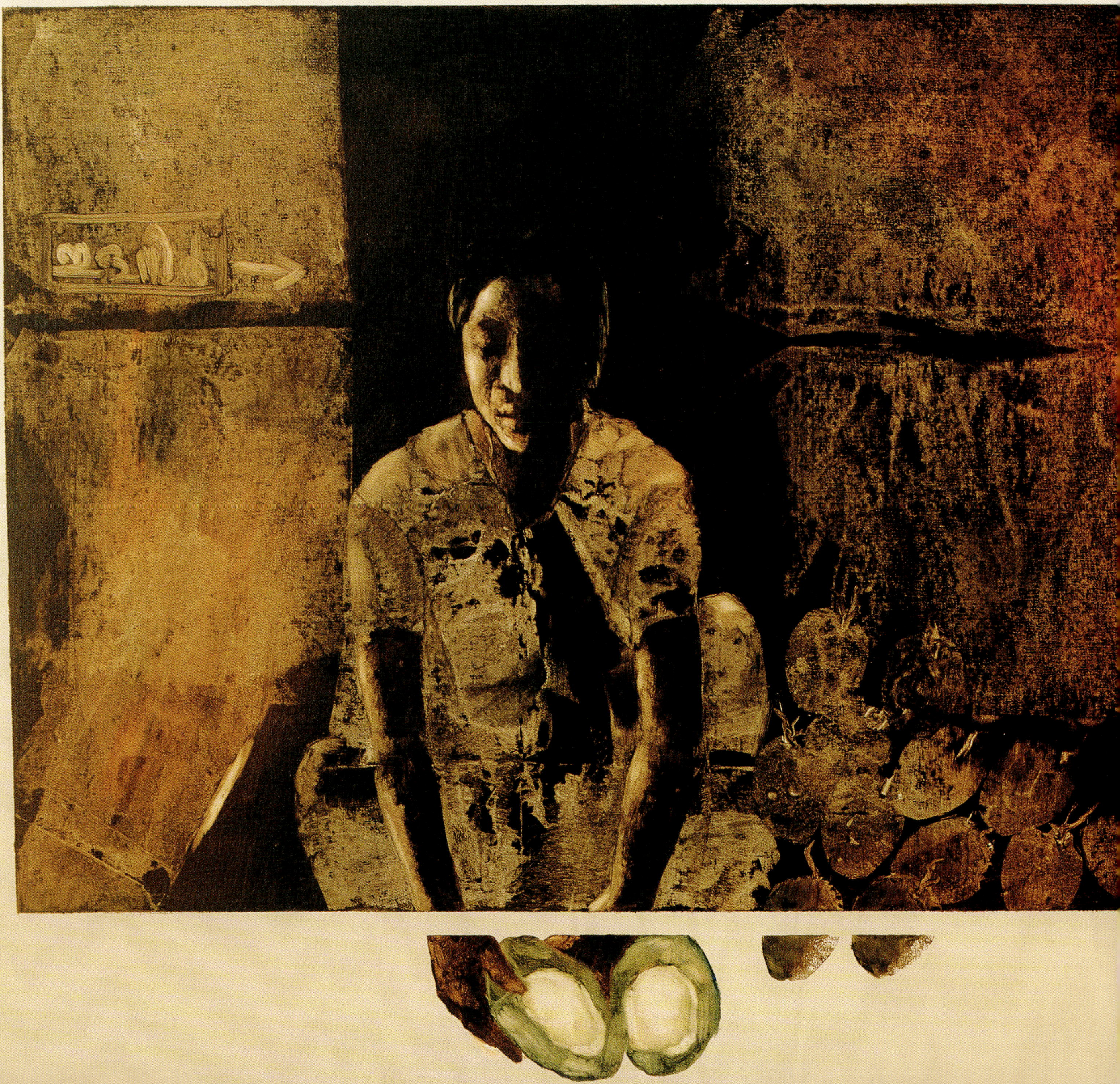

◀ The coconut seller
137 x 91.5 cm, oil on canvas, 2001

▶A *chaya kada*, wayside teashop
137 x 91.5 cm, oil on canvas, 2001

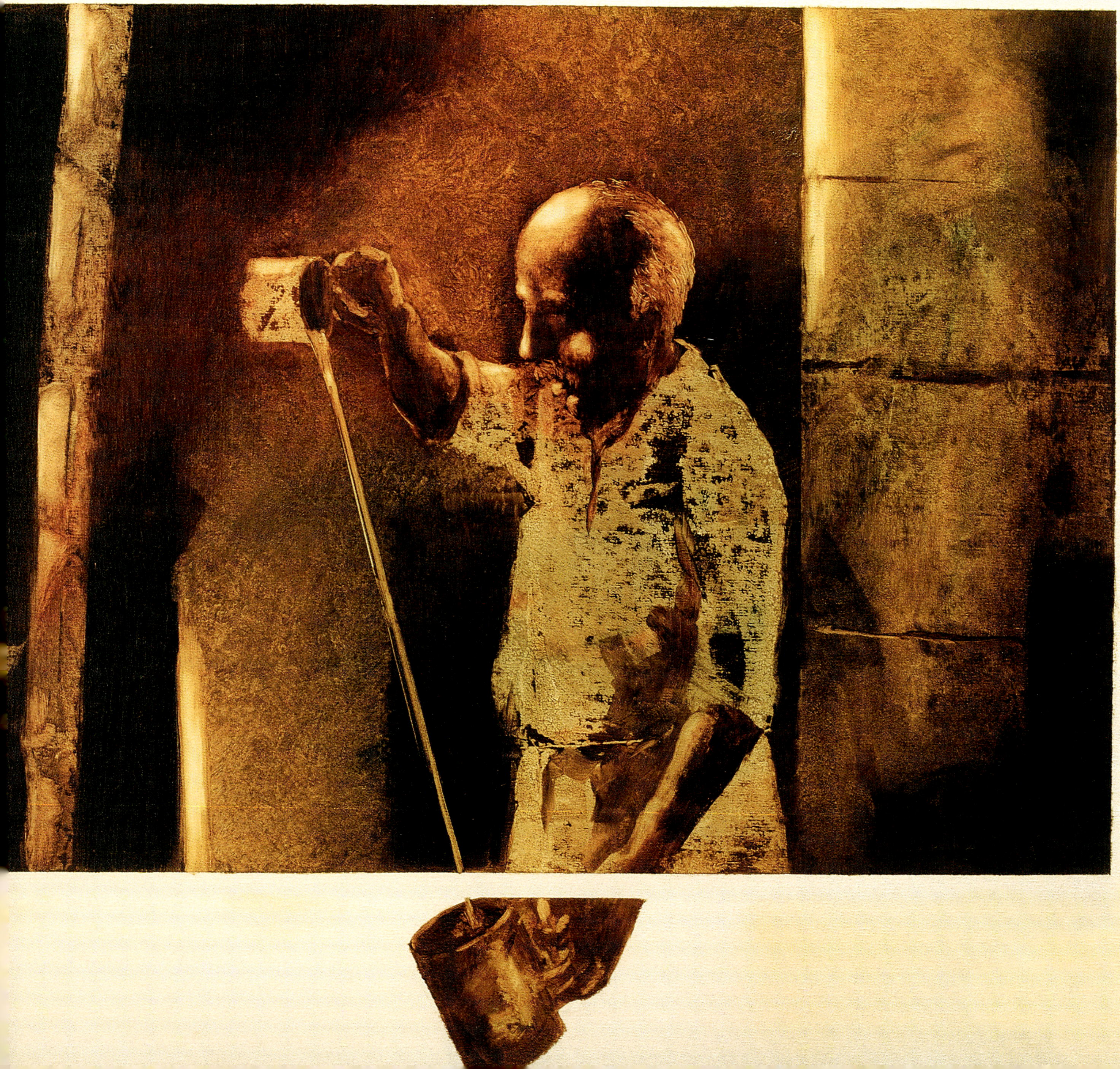

◀ Boatman Vinod at Pookode Lake
 10" x 14", pen and ink drawing, 2001

▶ A houseboat, Alapuzha
 10" x 14", pen and ink drawing, 2001

HOUSEBOAT ALAPPY.

41

◀ Fisherman, Kappad Beach
10" x 14", pen and ink drawing, 2001

▶ Vishnu Namboodiri, Palakkad
10" x 14", pen and ink drawing, 2001

Vishnu Namboodiri
Palakkad.

43

House Boat
KUTTANAD

◀ Houseboat, Alapuzha
10" x 14", watercolour, 2001

◀ Fish seller, Kollam
10" x 14", watercolour, 2001

▶ Mariamma, Kunnamkulam
10" x 14", watercolour, 2001

MARIAMA KUNNAMKULAM.

▶The backwaters
137 x 91.5 cm, oil on canvas, 2001

49

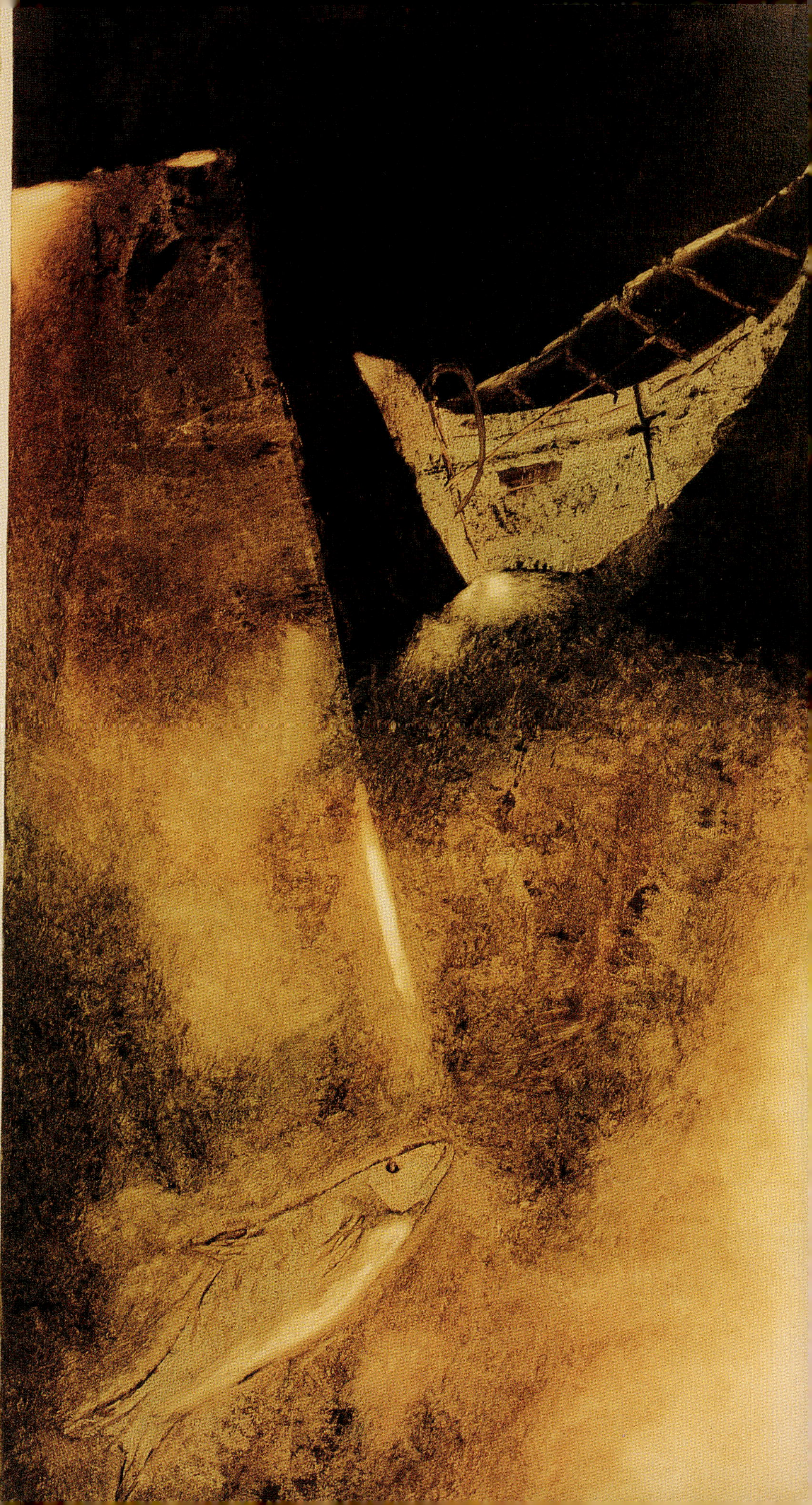

◀ A fisherman and his boat
137 x 183 cm, oil on canvas, 2001

▶ Karanvar, the family head
137 x 183 cm, oil on canvas, 2001

53

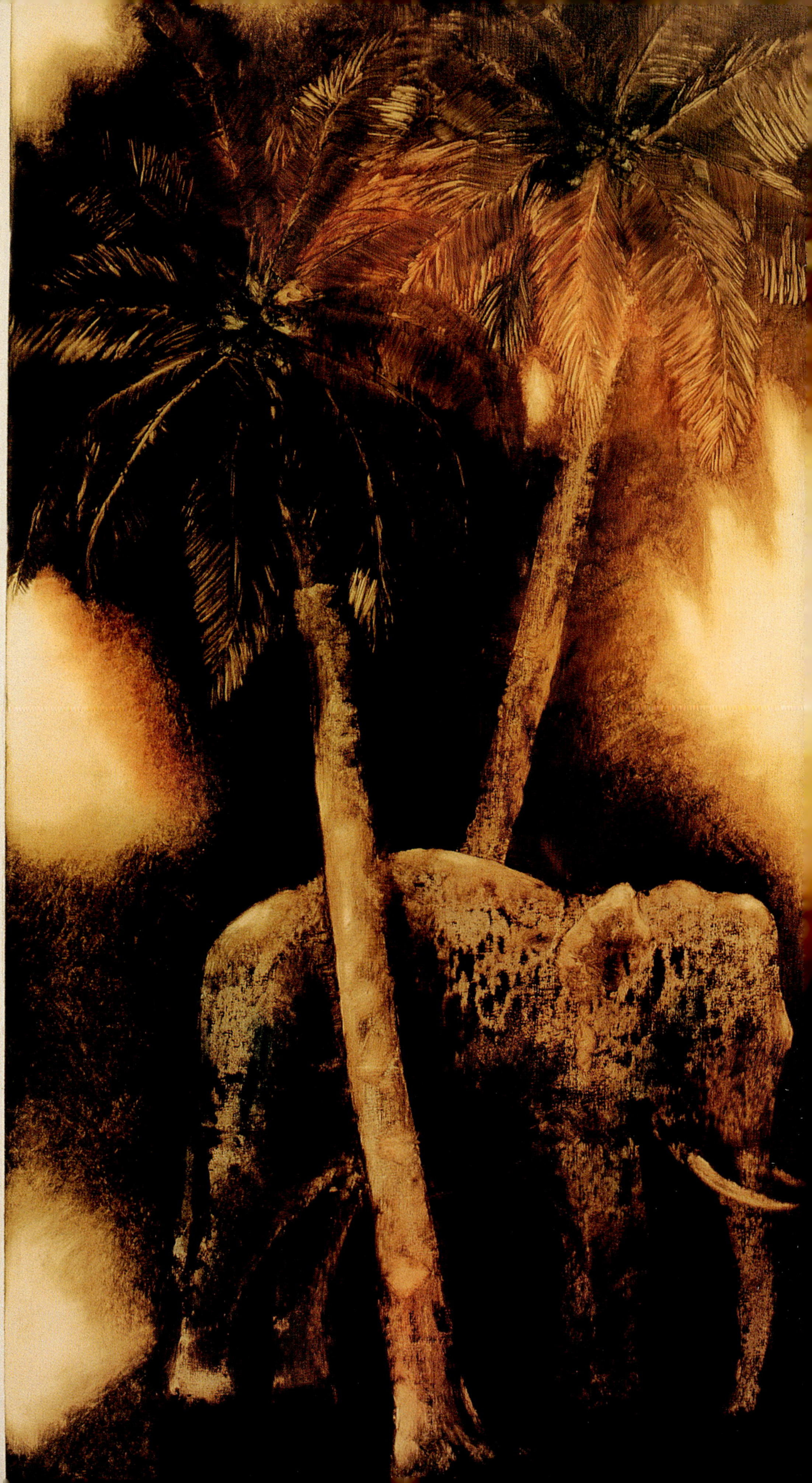

◀ Thekkady
137 x 183 cm, oil on canvas, 2001

◀ A catamaran
137 x 91.5 cm, oil on canvas, 2001

▶ The fishmonger
137 x 91.5 cm, oil on canvas, 2001

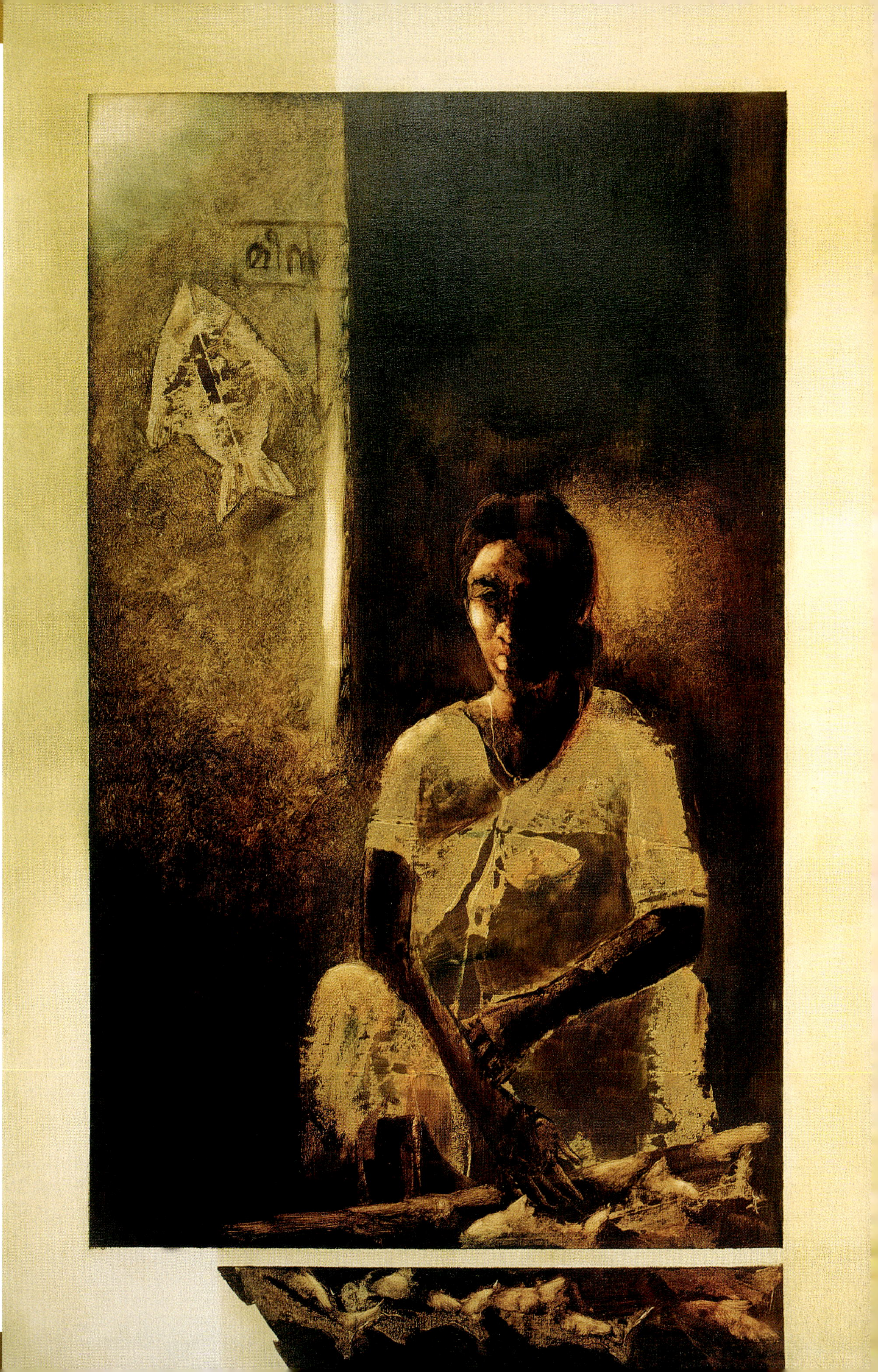

◀ Mopla girls
137 x 91.5 cm, oil on canvas, 2001

▶ A priest
137 x 91.5 cm, oil on canvas, 2001

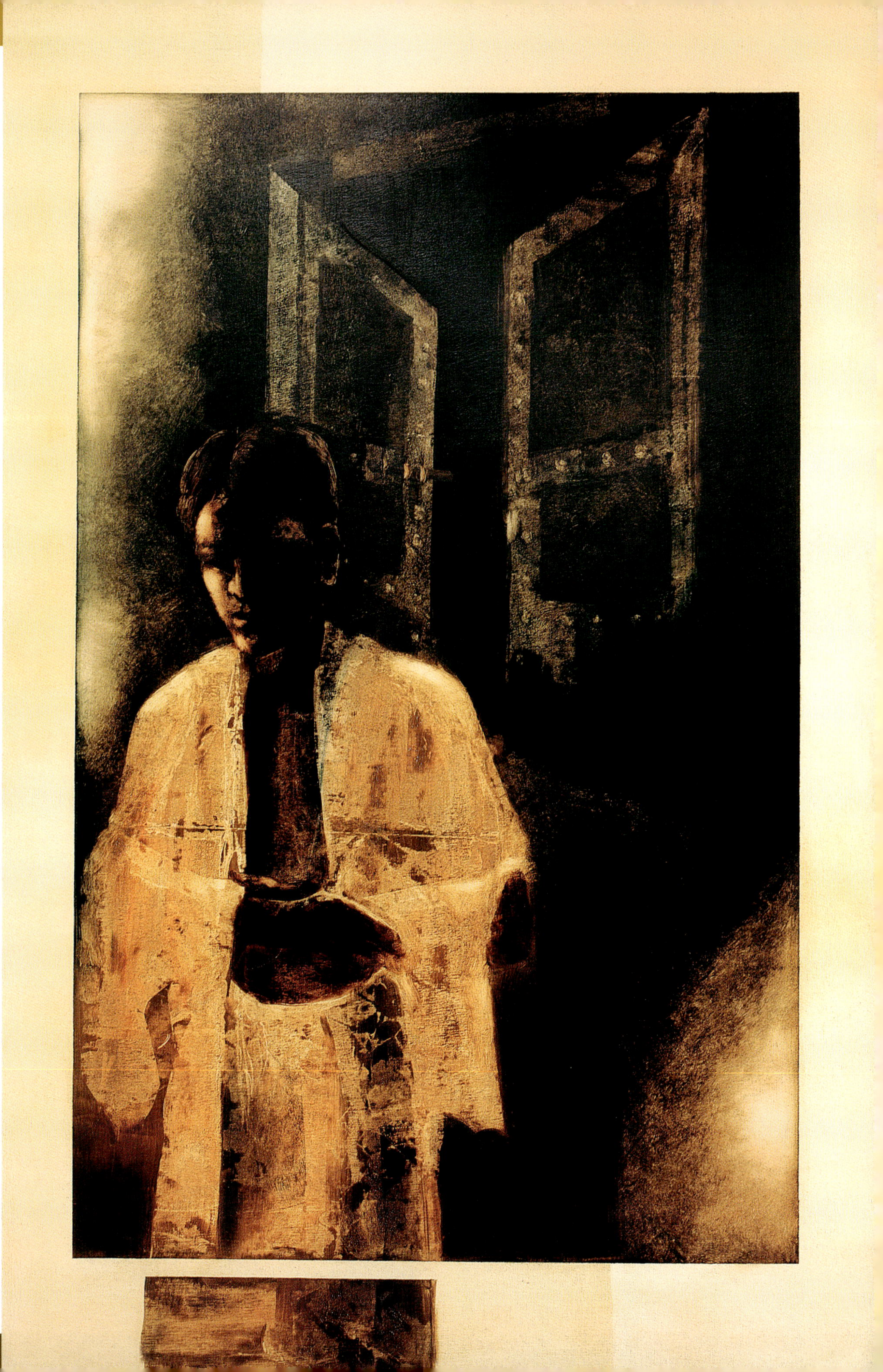

▲Portrait of man with multiethnic identity, Calicut
10" x 14", pen and ink drawing, 2001

▶Fisherman in a catamaran, Kovalam
  10" x 14", pen and ink drawing, 2001

SOMATHEERAM.

◀ Somatheeram Resort
10" x 14", pen and ink drawing, 2001

▲ Hameed, Kappad Beach
10" X 14", pen and ink drawing, 2001

◀ Catamaran, Kovalam Beach
10" x 14", pen and ink drawing, 2000

▶ A push carter, Calicut
10" x 14", pen and ink drawing, 2001

CALICUT-16.1.2001

▲ Marari Beach Resort, Mararikulam
10" x 14", pen and ink drawing, 2001

▶A Kuttanadan boat
  10" x 14", pen and ink drawing, 2001

◀ View from my cottage, Vythri
10" x 14", watercolour, 2001

▶ Sorting out chillies, Calicut
10" x 14', watercolour, 2001

Calicut 15-1-2001

Sorting out Chilli

ARAKKAL KETTU
CANNUR. 13-1-2001

▶ The young child who asked me to sketch him at Kappad Beach
10" X 14", pen and ink drawing, 2001

◀ Arakkal Kettu Palace, Kannaur
10" x 14", pen and ink drawing, 2001

◀ Vythri Resort
10" x 14", pen and ink drawing, 2001

▶ Houseboat, Alapuzha
10" x 14", pen and ink drawing, 2001

HOUSEBOAT ALAPPY.

◀ A typical Kuttanadan vessel
   10" x 14", pen and ink drawing, 2001

▶ Old warehouses, Alapuzha
   10" x 14", pen and ink drawing, 2001

OLD GODOWN ALAPPUZHA.

◀ Rukmini Nair, Pattambi
10" x 14", watercolour, 2001

▶ Abu, a loader, Chowghat
10" x 14", watercolour, 2001

ABU, LOADER
CHOWSHAT.

VYTHIRI RESORT

▶ Annamma, Wynad
   10" x 14", pen and ink drawing, 2001

◀ Vythri Resort
   10" x 14", pen and ink drawing, 2001

▶ A houseboat
10" x 14", pen and ink drawing, 2001

80

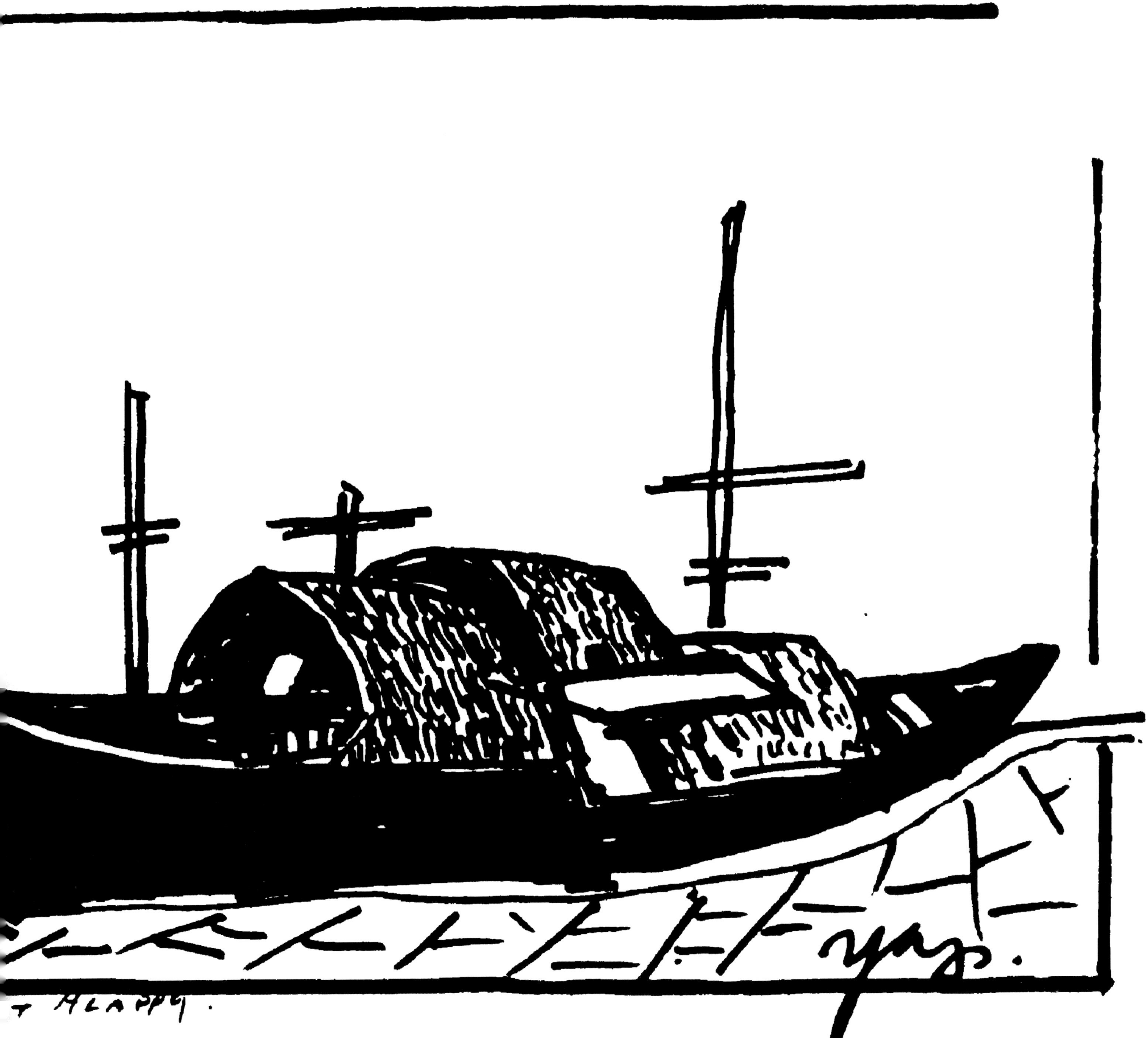
T ALAPPY.

◀ The Arab lineage
   10" x 14", pen and ink drawing, 2001

▶ Boatman Koya, Pookode Lake
   10" x 14", pen and ink drawing, 2001

Boatman Kunchikoya
Pookode Lake
12·1·2001

◀ Mopla girls coming out of
a tutorial, Kannaur
10" x 14", pen and ink drawing, 2001

▶ Beypore shipbuilding yard
10" x 14", pen and ink drawing, 2001

Beypore shipbuilding.   15-1-2001

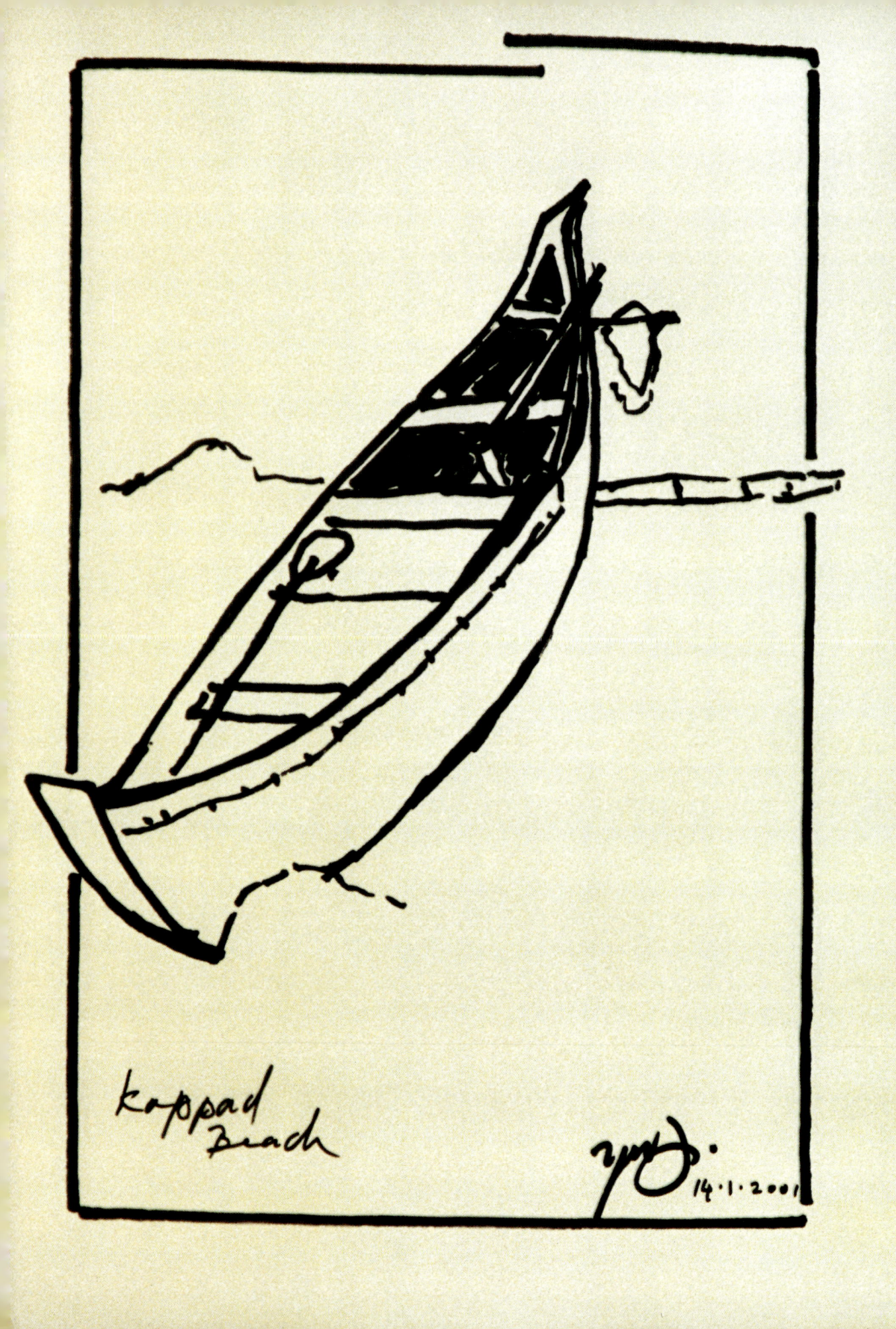

◀ Fishing boat, Kappad Beach
10" x 14", pen and ink drawing, 2001

▶ A Muslim woman, Malapuram
10" x 14", pen and ink drawing, 2001

AYISHA.
NALAPURAM

◀ A room boy in traditional attire
at Marari Resort
10" x 14", pen and ink drawing, 2001

▶ A traditional boat, Beypore
10" x 14", pen and ink drawing, 2001

14.2.2001

Beypore

BEYPORE
SHIPBUILDING

◀ Beypore traditional shipbuilding yard
10" x 14", watercolour, 2001

13-1-2001 Thalakkal Fort
KANNUR.

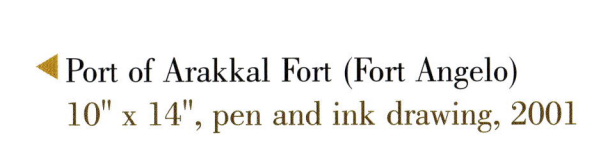

◀ Port of Arakkal Fort (Fort Angelo)
 10" x 14", pen and ink drawing, 2001

◀ Fisherman, Mararikulam
10" x 14", pen and ink drawing, 2001

◀ Port of Arakkal Fort (Fort Angelo)
10" x 14", pen and ink drawing, 2001

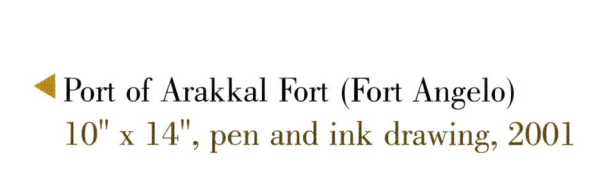

◀ Fisherman, Mararikulam
10" x 14", pen and ink drawing, 2001